MY FAVORITE PET
CHINCHILLAS

Victoria Marcos

xist Publishing

Published proudly in the State of Texas, USA by Xist Publishing
www.xistpublishing.com
24200 Southwest Freeway Suite 402- 290 Rosenberg, TX 77471

First Edition
Hardcover ISBN: 978-1-5324-1642-2
Paperback ISBN: 978-1-5324-1641-5
eISBN: 978-1-5324-1640-8
Printed in the United States of America

Table of Contents

My favorite pets are chinchillas. Would you like to learn about them?

Chinchillas live in cages in their owner's home.

They like to hide and sleep during the day. They prefer places that are very quiet. Chinchillas are mostly awake at night. They like to eat and play when it is dark.

Chinchillas have very soft fur. They have large eyes, round ears, and bushy tails. Their tails help them to keep their balance when they run and jump. They are very high jumpers, and can jump over six feet into the air.

Do You Remember?

When do chinchillas sleep?

Check and see if you're right at
the end of this book!

Chinchillas bathe in volcanic ash to keep their fur clean. They like to be clean and need to bathe once or twice a week. Chinchillas will jump into the ash and roll around, and it looks like they are having a lot of fun.

Chinchillas like to run on a wheel in their cages to get exercise. They need to be kept cool, because if they get too hot, they can get sick. Chinchillas have a hard time cooling down because they aren't able to sweat.

Chinchillas are very smart and can be taught to play with humans. However, they get scared easily. They move very quickly and are nervous animals.

Do You Remember?

How do chinchillas clean their fur?

Check and see if you're right at
the end of this book!

Chinchillas make many different sounds. When they're calm and happy, they will coo.
They chirp when they are exploring new places.

Chinchillas will make a barking sound when they feel threatened. They will bark a few times to warn other chinchillas of danger. They also bark when they feel nervous, or even if they have a bad dream or feel lonely.

Chinchillas are mostly herbivores.
They usually eat grass hay and
food pellets from the pet store.

They also like to eat nuts, dried
fruit, carrots, and
green vegetables.

Chinchillas hold their food with their front paws when they eat. They drink water from a water bottle in their cages.

Do You Remember?

What do chinchillas usually eat?

Check and see if you're right at
the end of this book!

Their teeth never stop growing and can grow two to three inches per year. Chinchillas chew on wood and hard food to keep their teeth from growing too much. If you take very good care of your pet chinchilla, it can live for about ten years.

What is your favorite
thing about Chinchillas?

Glossary

Balance: To remain upright and steady

Volcanic: Made by a volcano

Ash: What is left after something burns

Herbivore: An animal that eats plants

Threatened: Made to feel unsafe

Active: To move around a lot

Did You Remember?

Answers:
Question #1:
During the day
Question #2:
They roll around in volcanic ash
Question #3:
Chinchillas usually eat grass hay and
food pellets from the pet store

CPSIA information can be obtained
at www.ICGtesting.com
Printed in the USA
BVHW022310191021
619307BV00018B/364

9 781532 416415